Afternoon at the Seaside

A play

Agatha Christie

Samuel French — London
New York - Toronto - Hollywood

© 1963 BY AGATHA CHRISTIE

1. This play is fully protected under the Copyright Laws of the British Commonwealth of Nations, the United States of America and all countries of the Berne and Universal Copyright Conventions.

2. All rights, including Stage, Motion Picture, Radio, Television, Public Reading, and Translation into Foreign Languages, are strictly reserved.

3. No part of this publication may lawfully be reproduced in ANY form or by any means—photocopying, typescript, recording (including video-recording), manuscript, electronic, mechanical, or otherwise—or be transmitted or stored in a retrieval system, without prior permission.

Rights of Performance by Amateurs are controlled by SAMUEL FRENCH LTD, 52 FITZROY STREET, LONDON W1T 5JR, and they, or their authorized agents, issue licences to amateurs on payment of a fee. It is an infringement of the Copyright to give any performance or public reading of the play before the fee has been paid and the licence issued.

5. Licences are issued subject to the understanding that it shall be made clear in all advertising matter that the audience will witness an amateur performance; that the names of the authors of the plays shall be included on all announcements and on all programmes; and that the integrity of the author's work will be preserved.

The Royalty Fee indicated below is subject to contract and subject to variation at the sole discretion of Samuel French Ltd.

Basic fee for each and every
performance by amateurs   Code F
in the British Isles

In Theatres or Halls seating Four Hundred or more the fee will be subject to negotiation.

In Territories Overseas the fee quoted above may not apply. A fee will be quoted on application to our local authorized agent, or if there is no such agent, on application to Samuel French Ltd, London.

The publication of this play does not imply that it is necessarily available for performance by amateurs or professionals, either in the British Isles or Overseas. Amateurs and professionals considering a production are strongly advised in their own interests to apply to the appropriate agents for consent before starting rehearsals or booking a theatre or hall.

ISBN 0 573 02004 3

AFTERNOON AT THE SEASIDE

Presented by Peter Saunders at the Duchess Theatre, London, on the 20th December 1962, with the following cast of characters:

(in the order of their appearance)

BOB WHEELER	*David Langton*
NOREEN SOMERS	*Betty McDowall*
ARTHUR SOMERS	*Michael Beint*
GEORGE CRUM	*Robert Raglan*
MRS CRUM	*Mabelle George*
A MOTHER	*Vera Cook*
A YOUNG MAN	*John Quayle*
BEACH ATTENDANT	*John Abineri*
MRS GUNNER (MOM)	*Margot Boyd*
PERCY GUNNER	*Raymond Bowers*
THE BEAUTY	*Mercy Haystead*
INSPECTOR FOLEY	*Robin May*

Directed by HUBERT GREGG

Setting by PETER RICE

SCENE: *The beach at Little-Slippyng-on-Sea*

Time—a summer afternoon

AFTERNOON AT THE SEASIDE

SCENE—*The beach. A summer afternoon.*

Three bathing huts face the audience on a rostrum. That on the right is labelled BIDE-A-WEE. *The middle one is* MON DESIR, *that on the left* BEN NEVIS. *In front of the huts is an asphalted walk reached by a ramp and three steps up* L. *Extreme* R *is a beach telescope for viewing the bay. In the foreground, below the rostrum and reached by short sets of steps before each hut, is an assortment of beach litter, banana skins, empty cigarette cartons, odd bathing towels, a shrimping net and an abandoned sand castle. To* L *of these is a deck chair.*

As the CURTAIN *rises, or just before, voices are heard singing "I do like to be beside the seaside," rather out of tune.*

When the CURTAIN *rises, the lights fade up from a* BLACK-OUT. *The doors of* MON DESIR *and* BEN NEVIS *are closed, but* BIDE-A-WEE *is open and shows itself full of equipment, cups, etc., on hooks, coats, folded table and chairs—in fact quite a home from home. In front of it, in two canvas upright chairs, sit* MR *and* MRS CRUM. GEORGE *sits* R *and* MRS CRUM, L. MR CRUM *is elderly, fat and outwardly submissive to* MRS CRUM, *who is fifty-two, loquacious and generally censorious. She is knitting and he is trying to read the local afternoon paper. On the beach* L, *roughly in front of* BEN NEVIS, MRS SOMERS *and* BOB WHEELER *are sprawling on the sands in bathing dresses.* NOREEN SOMERS *is a good-looking, rather blowsy woman of thirty-odd with enormous vivacity.* BOB WHEELER *is about the same age, a terrific wag, and sure to be the life and soul of any gathering.* MR SOMERS *is sitting in a deck-chair* L, *wearing an overcoat and scarf, with a heavy stick propped by him. He looks grey and tired. A heap of clothes lies by these three where they have undressed on the beach—grey flannel trousers, cotton frock, slip, etc.* NOREEN SOMERS *is adorning a large and handsome sand castle with cockle shells. Off* L *a small child is bawling at the top of his voice. Dogs are barking intermittently.*

BOB (*removing a bucket from the top of the sand castle*) There you are.

NOREEN. There's a clever boy.

BOB. A fairy castle for the girl of my dreams.

NOREEN. Better not let Arthur hear you.

BOB. He's asleep.

NOREEN. Just as well.

BOB. Girl of my dreams, I love you. (*He takes a sweet from a chocolate box and eats it*) Honest, I do.

NOREEN. Hey, that was my last soft centre. (*She throws the box on the sand R of Bob*)

BOB (*taking the box and throwing it towards a little bin R*) Ay, ay. Keep Britain tidy.

(*A jet aeroplane is heard flying overhead, followed by the barking of a dog*)

NOREEN. Any more shells?

BOB (*picking up a shell from the sand*) Here you are, Noreen. Here's a beauty.

(*A MOTHER enters R, crossing to L*)

MOTHER. Ernie! Ernie! Stop it, I say! (*To Bob, at his R*) No, not you. I'm talking to my son. Leave that dog alone —it'll bite you! (*She stands by the exit down L*)

NOREEN. Ta, ever so.

(*A beach ball bounces on from L, followed by a YOUNG MAN, who clambers over the people on the sand for the ball, and exits L*)

YOUNG MAN. Sorry. Sorry. Sorry.

MOTHER. Ernie!

BOB. Never a dull moment at the seaside, that's what I always say.

MOTHER. Why don't you go and have a paddle? Look at Bert, he's paddling. Why don't you go and paddle too?

CHILD (*off*) Don't wanna paddle—wah!

MOTHER. Bring you to the seaside I do to enjoy yourself, and what happens? You bawl your head off.

CHILD (*off*) Don't want to—wah!

MOTHER. Well, I'm going to enjoy myself if it's the last thing I do.

CHILD (*off*) *Waaah!*

MOTHER. Oh, shut up! (*She crosses R, above Bob*)

BOB. Kids, eh?

MOTHER (*turning and looking at Bob*) What! ! ! (*She turns away*)

(*The* MOTHER *exits* R)

NOREEN. First time I went to the seaside I yelled my head off. Said the sea was wet and the sand was dirty You never enjoy a thing first time you do it.

BOB. That's right. Goes for other things than the seaside, eh, Norrie?

NOREEN. Now, Bob, steady! You'll shock Arthur here.

BOB (*looking at Mr Somers, who does not react at all*) Couldn't shock old Arthur. Nothing shocks Arthur, does it, Artie?

(MR SOMERS *merely smiles in a tired way*)

NOREEN (*kneeling and taking a bathing-cap from her beach-bag*) Oh, well, I'm going in for my second dip. Come on, Bob.

BOB. Too bloomin' cold.

NOREEN. Slacker!

BOB. Women don't feel the cold. (*Eyeing her*) Too well covered. (*He smacks her bottom*)

NOREEN. You give over. (*She rises*) I'll race you to the jetty.

BOB (*rising to the ramp* L) Right. On your marks. Get set. (*He runs off down* L)

NOREEN (*following him*) Hey, you cheated!

(BOB *and* NOREEN *exit down* L.

MR SOMERS *rises, puts down his newspaper, picks up his stick, and goes up the ramp and steps to exit off up* L)

MRS CRUM (*watching in disapproval*) I must say, George, that Little-Slippyng isn't what it was.

GEORGE. Little-Slippyng slipping, eh?

MRS CRUM. *Quite* a different class of people nowadays. I've a good mind not to come here next year.

GEORGE. Ar . . .

MRS CRUM. Talking and screaming and making those very doubtful jokes! Just as though they were alone on the beach.

GEORGE. Needn't listen, my dear.

MRS CRUM. What did you say?

GEORGE. Said you needn't listen.

MRS CRUM (*sharply*) Don't talk nonsense, George.

GEORGE. No, my dear.

MRS CRUM. And that one with all the jokes isn't even her husband. It's the other one she's married to.

GEORGE. How do you know?

(*The beach ball comes in from* L *right on to the rostrum. The* YOUNG MAN *follows it*)

MRS CRUM. Well, really!

YOUNG MAN. Sorry. (*He retrieves the ball*)

(*The* YOUNG MAN *exits* L)

MRS CRUM. Mothers who can't control their children! Young men and girls with next to nothing on, kicking balls all over the place. No consideration for those who want to sit peacefully and enjoy themselves.

GEORGE. Only young once.

MRS CRUM. That's a foolish thing to say—very foolish indeed.

GEORGE. Yes, dear.

MRS CRUM. We didn't behave like that when we were young. (*She leans over to take wool from the bag at the side of her chair*) And in my mother's day, men and girls bathed from different beaches even.

GEORGE. That can't have been much fun.

MRS CRUM (*sitting up*) What did you say?

GEORGE. Nothing, dear. Nothing at all. Seems there was a burglary here last night.

MRS CRUM. At Little-Slippyng?

GEORGE. Yes. Lady Beckman.

MRS CRUM. What—the Lady Beckman that has all those mink coats and the lovely Rollses? Is she down here?

GEORGE. Esplanade Hotel.

MRS CRUM. What was taken—a mink coat?

GEORGE. No. Emerald necklace.

MRS CRUM. An . . . ? (*Sitting up*) Oh? (*She resumes knitting*) Oh, well, I dare say she's got half a dozen of those, too. I wonder she even noticed it was gone!

(MR SOMERS *enters down the ramp* L, *moves to his deck-chair, and sits*)

GEORGE. Cat burglar, they think. Got in through the

bathroom window after crawling up a drainpipe while the dancing was going on in the evening.

MRS CRUM. Serves her right!

(*The* BEACH ATTENDANT, *a very old man in uniform, with rheumy eyes and a red nose, enters down* L *to above Mr Somers*)

BEACH ATTENDANT. Fourpence, please. (*He takes off his cap, wipes his head, and replaces the cap*)

(MR SOMERS *is busy reading a magazine*)

Fourpence for the chair.

MR SOMERS. Oh! (*He finds a florin*)

(*The* BEACH ATTENDANT *punches a ticket, gives it to Mr Somers, takes the florin from him*)

Nice afternoon—quite warm.

(*The* BEACH ATTENDANT *gets change from his money bag and counts it into Mr Somers's hand*)

BEACH ATTENDANT. Sixpence, shillin', two shillin's. (*Gloomily*) Too nice an afternoon makes a lot of trouble. You should see the parking lot! Regular mix up! Some of them cars won't get out for hours.

MR SOMERS. Isn't there someone to control it?

BEACH ATTENDANT. Ah—old Joe—but it's more than one man can manage. Cars coming in in a stream ever since lunch-time and parking themselves where they please. Ah, I remember this place when there wasn't more than a couple of dozen on the beach—all residents they were—quiet and well be'aved . . . (*He breaks off, looking off* L, *and suddenly yells*) Hey—you! Stop throwin' stones, you'll 'it someone! (*To Mr Somers and the world*) Boys! Always up to something. (*He looks out front, looks at his watch, and blows his whistle*) Hey, you—float number twelve—you've 'ad your half-hour! Come in! (*He pauses*) Eh?

(*The* BEACH ATTENDANT *exits* R, *blowing his whistle*)

MRS CRUM (*her hands to her ears*) That whistle.

(*The beach ball bounds on from* L *and hits George. The* YOUNG MAN *enters from* L, *even more out of breath*)

YOUNG MAN. Sorry! (*He retrieves the ball and throws it off* L)

(*There is an agonized protest from* MRS GUNNER ("MOM") *off* L)

Sorry.

(*The* YOUNG MAN *exits* L.
MOM *enters* L *as the Young Man exits, brushing sand off herself. She is a possessive old battle-axe.* PERCY, *her son, follows her on. He is a nice but sad young man*)

MOM. Well, I don't know what the young are coming to! (*She goes up the ramp to* R *of Ben Nevis*)

(PERCY *follows Mom to her* L)

I really don't! Sand all over me! Now, Percy, open the house. (*She gives the key to Percy*)

(PERCY *opens the hut, takes out Mom's chair and puts it* R *of the hut*)

MRS CRUM. Good afternoon, Mrs Gunner.
MOM. Good afternoon, Mrs Crum. Good afternoon, Mr Crum.

(GEORGE *raises his hat, still reading*)

PERCY (*placing the chair facing front*) Here you are, Mom. Which way would you like it?
MOM. That's very nice, thank you, dear. (*She sits*)

(PERCY *brings out his chair, and puts it* L *of the hut*)

No, I think I'll have it a bit more round. (*She rises*)

(PERCY *moves her chair to face farther* L. MOM *sits.* PERCY *sits*)

And my knitting.

(PERCY *rises, brings her knitting and a towel out of the hut, places the towel on his chair and the knitting on Mom's* L)

That's it. On the other side.

(PERCY *moves the knitting to* R *of Mom.* MOM *puts her bag on her* L. PERCY *gives her the key, and sits. Quite a business is made of it all*)

(*Fondly*) He's such a good son to me.

(PERCY *is embarrassed*)

Not that I want to keep him always waiting on me. "You must leave me and go and enjoy yourself," I say. We old women must expect to sit back and take second place. He wouldn't go to the pictures last night because he thought I had a bit of a headache.

MRS CRUM. That's nice. That's very nice. That's what I like to hear.

GEORGE. *Did* you have a headache?

MOM (*with dignity*) It passed off. (*She sorts out her knitting*)

GEORGE. I'll bet it did. It was never damned well there in the first place.

(MRS CRUM *glares at George, who stops*)

YOUNG MAN (*off* L) Per-cie. Per-cie—come on—we've been waiting for you.

PERCY (*rising to the edge of the rostrum*) Hy!

MOM. Who's that, dear? (*Shading her eyes*) I can't see.

PERCY. It's Edie and Tom.

MOM. Edie—is that the red-haired girl who wanted you to go on the charabanc trip?

PERCY (*moving down the ramp*) That's right—that's Edie. They've got a boat.

(PERCY *goes off down* L)

MOM. I don't think there's time for that today, Percy.

(PERCY *re-enters, standing down* L)

I might want you to get me another skein of wool before the shops shut.

PERCY (*standing down* L) Well—I kind of promised . . .

MOM (*martyred*) Of *course* go if you want to, dear. I never want to stand in the way of you enjoying yourself. I know only too well what a trouble we old people are.

PERCY (*crossing up to Mom*) Oh, look here, Mom . . .

MOM. I dare say I can manage to get to the shops myself —if it's not too hot. It's just I feel my heart a little.

(GEORGE *blows his nose*)

PERCY. No, no. I'll get your wool. I don't know that I
want to go out in the boat.

MOM. You don't really like going on the sea, do you,
dear? Even as a little boy, you weren't a good sailor.

PERCY. It's calm enough today. I'd better tell them.

(PERCY *exits down* L, *dejected*)

MOM (*with satisfaction*) I knew he didn't really want to go.
Percy's so good-natured—and these girls just badger a man
so that he doesn't like to refuse. That Edie now—quite the
wrong type for Percy.

MRS CRUM. It's lucky he's got you to look after him.

MOM. Yes. Now if a really nice girl came along, I'd be
only too pleased for Percy to be friendly with her.

GEORGE. Would you?

MOM (*with a delightful laugh*) Oh, yes. Nothing of the
grudging mother about *me*. Some mothers can't bear their
sons to go about with other people. I'm only too pleased. I
wish Percy would do it more. But he's so devoted to me
that I really can't persuade him to leave me. "You're better
company than any girl, Mom," he says. Ridiculous, isn't it?

GEORGE. Yes.

MRS CRUM (*glaring at George, and smiling at Mum*) Ah,
there's a lot of truth in the old saying that a boy's best
friend is his mother.

(*The* BEAUTY *steps out of Mon Desir. She is a true pin-up
girl. She is wearing a daring Bikini and a good deal of make-up,
and looks very exotic and slightly foreign. She has an elaborate
bag and a vanity case. Possibly a beach wrap with "Je t'aime,
I love you, Ich liebe dich," etc., patterned all over it. She turns to
close the door.*

MRS CRUM *and* MOM *look her up and down*)

BEAUTY (*after standing for a moment, seemingly unconscious of
all around her, but with a suggestion of a model posing*) Mesdames,
Messieurs, good afternoon! (*She goes down on to the sand and
sits* C)

(MRS CRUM *and* MOM *look at each other, then at Beauty*)

MOM. French!!

(*They knit.*
GEORGE *leans forward to stare goggle-eyed.* MR SOMERS

also cranes his neck round and stares. BEAUTY *takes out a cigarette-case from her bag, and a lighter which will not light.* GEORGE *and* MR SOMERS *rise to her assistance.* GEORGE *lights her cigarette. The men exchange a look)*

BEAUTY *(to George; with a breath-taking smile and a slight accent)* Oh, thank you. You are so kind.

GEORGE *(incoherent)* Not at all—not at all—pleasure.

(The men start to return. BEAUTY *drops her lighter.* MR SOMERS *reaches it and hands it to her.* GEORGE *looks on)*

BEAUTY *(transferring her smile to Mr Somers)* Oh, but I am stupid. Thank you very much.

MR SOMERS. Delighted—no trouble . . .

(The men exchange a look, and return to their seats)

MRS CRUM *(coldly)* What's on at the Pier Pavilion to-night, George?

GEORGE *(still goggling at Beauty)* Yes?

MRS CRUM. George, didn't you hear me?

GEORGE. Eh? What?

MRS CRUM. I—said—what's—on—at—the—Pavilion?

GEORGE *(flustered, looking at the paper)* Oh—yes—*The Woman Tempted Me.* *(He looks at Beauty, at Mrs Crum, then away)*

(There is a slight pause, then BEAUTY *rises, discards her wrap, and places it and the beach bag on the rostrum.*
The ball bounces on. BEAUTY *fends it off.*
The YOUNG MAN *enters, sees her and begins to dither.*
BEAUTY *laughs)*

YOUNG MAN *(L of Beauty)* I'm ever so sorry. I am—reely.

BEAUTY. But it is quite all right. It did not hurt me.

YOUNG MAN. Oh, oh, I wouldn't—not for the world—are you sure?

BEAUTY *(smiling at him)* Why, yes, I am quite sure.

GIRL'S VOICE *(off L)* Fred!

YOUNG MAN. Oh, coming! *(Explaining to Beauty)* My sister.

GIRL'S VOICE. Fred!

YOUNG MAN. Coming!

(*The* YOUNG MAN *goes off* L, *holding the ball, staring at Beauty with his head over his shoulder, and tripping over the ramp.*
    BEAUTY *bends and picks up a shell*)

MRS CRUM. George!

(GEORGE *gives her a guilty look and pretends to read the newspaper, watching Beauty from behind it.*
    BEAUTY *exits* R)

MOM. Those Bikinis, as they call them. Didn't ought to be allowed. The Archbishop of Canterbury should preach against them.
MRS CRUM. No *nice* girl would wear one.

(PERCY *enters slowly* L, *depressed*)

MOM (*brightly*) Seen your friends off?
PERCY (*sadly*) Yes, they've gone. (*He looks off* L *to the sea*) I'll go and get your wool now. (*He starts up the ramp*)
MOM. I think—after all—I shall have just enough.
GEORGE. You bloody well would have.

(MRS CRUM *glares at George and gives an embarrassed laugh to Mom.* GEORGE *rises, moves to the telescope* R, *focuses in the direction Beauty has gone, and takes some money from his pocket*)

MRS CRUM. Don't waste your money, George.

(GEORGE *re-focuses the telescope*)

GEORGE. There was a ship out there. No, dear. (*He sits*)
MOM. You'd better have your afternoon dip, Percy.
PERCY. Don't think I want to. (*He crosses to* R *of the steps* C) It's turning cold. The sun's nearly off the beach.
MOM. Oh, but it's good for you, Percy. This is your holiday, you know. You want to enjoy yourself.
PERCY. Not much fun going in by yourself.
MOM. Now go along, dear. Needn't stop in long. The salt water's good for you.

(*Morosely,* PERCY *moves to near the deck-chair, taking off his shirt and trousers. He is wearing bathing costume underneath. The trousers lie close to those of Bob*)

MOM. Put your things in the hut.

PERCY (*still morose*) They're all right there. (*With his back to the ramp, he reaches for the towel on his chair*)

(NOREEN *rushes in from* L, *knocking Percy over.* BOB *follows her on*)

NOREEN. Oh, sorry, I'm sure. (*Giving him a coquettish glance*) Never look where I'm going.
PERCY. That's all right.
NOREEN. It's lovely and warm.
BOB. Don't believe her, chum. It's freezing. (*He runs "on the spot", then dries himself*)

(PERCY *goes off* L)

NOREEN (*drying herself*) Oh, you! Soft—that's what you are.
BOB (*crossing to her and showing his muscles*) Soft? Me? Feel those muscles.

(NOREEN *drops her towel.* BOB *picks her up, twirls her round, and they sit,* NOREEN L *of the sand castle,* BOB R *of it.* MOM *and* MRS CRUM *register aloof distaste*)

NOREEN (*kneeling, resting on Mr Somers's knees*) Oh, I'm all dizzy.
BOB. Oh! I've done myself an injury! (*He lies on his towel,* R *of the sand castle, with his head up stage*) How about a bit of sun on the body beautiful, eh? (*He beats a tattoo on his stomach*)

(NOREEN *settles down on the sand*)

MRS CRUM. Mrs Gunner . . .
MOM. Pardon?
MRS CRUM. Have you heard there was a burglary last night? That Lady Beckman who's always in the papers—the one with the minks—lost her emerald necklace.
MOM. I expect she took it herself—for the insurance. They're always doing that sort of thing.
GEORGE. Says in the paper here it was a cat burglar.
MRS CRUM. These cat burglars go all round the seaside resorts in summer. Do you remember, George, there was a burglary here last year—and *that* was a cat burglar.

(BOB *sits up*)

Some film star lost a diamond bracelet.

GEORGE (*sleepily*) Don't remember.

MRS CRUM. Oh, you must remember. It made ever such a stir. There were pictures of the window and the drain-pipe and lots of pictures of her and bits about a new picture she was going to do.

GEORGE (*closing his eyes*) Nice bit of publicity.

(BOB *teases Noreen with a shell*)

NOREEN. You leave me alone, you great bully! (*She circles the sand castle and trips over Mom's feet*) Oh, sorry, I'm sure.

MOM. I've dropped a stitch.

NOREEN (*moving up the steps to Mom's L*) Oh, I say—(*helpfully*) let me pick it up for you.

MOM. No, thank you.

NOREEN. Oh, go on. I'm ever so good at picking up stitches.

MOM (*with venom*) No, certainly not.

BOB (*kneeling on all fours facing Mom*) No harm in being civil, is there?

MOM (*frostily*) I beg your pardon.

NOREEN (*moving down the steps and across to Mr Somers*) Leave it, Bob. Artie, got a cigarette? (*She takes two cigarettes from Mrs Somers's packet and lights them both*)

BOB. This place is like a bloomin' morgue. (*He rises, puts the bucket on his head, and does an Egyptian dance*)

NOREEN. Here, Bob, sit down.

(*A dog is heard barking*)

Have a cigarette.

(BOB *takes a cigarette and sits as before*)

MOTHER (*off R*) Ernie! Ernie! You ain't half a naughty boy. Ernie!

(*The dog stops barking*)

NOREEN. Wish I'd brought my transistor. We could have had a bit of Adam.

BOB. That stuff's on the way out. Give me the old minstrels. (*He sings*) Oh, I do like to be beside the sea side——

NOREEN. —I do like to be beside the sea——
BOB. I do like to stroll along the prom—prom—prom——
NOREEN }
BOB   } (*singing together*) Where the brass band plays
                                tiddley-om-pom-pom——
BOB. —Oh, I——
GEORGE (*singing*) —do like to be beside the seaside! I do like . . . (*He breaks off*)

(MRS CRUM *glares at George.*
A jet plane passes over from L *to* R)

BOB. How'd you like to be up there, Noreen? Two-seater jet.
NOREEN. Don't talk so daft, Bob. You'd be scared to death. You know you would.

(INSPECTOR FOLEY, *a tall, uniformed figure, enters down* R, *followed by the* BEACH ATTENDANT)

BOB. Scared? Scared be . . . (*He ad libs until* NOREEN *sees the Inspector*)
GEORGE. Why, it's Inspector Foley. Remember us from last year? Crum!
FOLEY (*nodding to him*) Good afternoon, Mr Crum—Mrs Crum.
GEORGE (*facetiously*) Well, how's crime?
FOLEY. Hoh! (*He crosses to* C, *mounts the steps of Mon Desir, and moves to* L *of Mrs Crum*)

(*The* BEACH ATTENDANT *remains down* R)

Or mustn't I ask, on your afternoon off?
MRS CRUM. This is Inspector Foley, Mrs Gunner.
FOLEY (*turning to Mom*) Good afternoon, madam. (*To George*) Unfortunately I'm *not* off duty, Mr Crum.
GEORGE (*taking off his spectacles*) Looking for cat burglars, is that it?
FOLEY. You're on the right track.
GEORGE. Doesn't seem much scope for them here. (*He looks at the huts*)
FOLEY. Information received, it seems some kids were out after dark last night and were down on the beach playing

cops and robbers, or spacemen and atom bombs or whatever kids do play nowadays, and they saw a man sneaking round the huts at this end of the Parade.

(BOB *nudges Noreen*)

I dare say they wouldn't have thought much of it but the man bolted when he saw them.

MRS CRUM. I suppose he was trying to steal something out of the huts?

FOLEY. According to them, he was trying to shove something *into* a hut through the little back window. The kids only came clean about it this afternoon. It might just possibly tie up with the theft of Lady Beckman's necklace. Passing it on to an accomplice.

BOB. Loverlee! (*Putting his hands up*) Search me, Officer, I am innocent.

MR SOMERS. Stop playing the fool, Bob.

BOB. Oh blimey, I thought you were dead. (*He turns to the others*) I thought he was dead.

(NOREEN *laughs*)

GEORGE. So you're searching all the huts?

FOLEY. Just the huts this end of the beach. We've done the first three. (*He points* R) It definitely wasn't farther along than the sixth.

GEORGE (*to Mrs Crum*) Didn't notice an emerald necklace, did you, Mother, in our palatial establishment?

MRS CRUM. Well, I never! Do you really think it might be in Bide-a-Wee? (*Pleased and flustered*) We've got so much stuff in there that I mightn't have noticed it. You go in and have a good look round, Inspector.

FOLEY (*coming down the steps of Mon Desir*) Thank you, Mrs Crum.

GEORGE. Anything in it for us, if you find it?

FOLEY (*mounting the steps of Bide-a-Wee, and going into the hut*) Reward of one thousand pounds offered by Sir Rupert Backman . . .

GEORGE. Not bad.

(PERCY *enters down* L *and moves on to the ramp*)

BOB. Might be a prison sentence if it's found in your hut —receiving stolen goods.

Mrs Crum. How dare you!

Percy. What's going on?

Bob. Hello, old boy. We're all under suspicion—particularly those who own beach huts.

Noreen. It's the emerald necklace that was stolen from Lady Beckman last night.

Mrs Crum. Someone was seen pushing it through one of the hut windows.

George. They don't know it *was* the necklace.

Bob. Might have been a love letter, or obscene literature.

Noreen. Really, Bob, your mind! (*She laughs*)

(Bob *laughs.* Percy *dries himself on his towel by his chair*)

Bob. Anyway, old girl, we're in the clear. (*He looks at Mrs Crum*) We're not one of the nobs with a beach hut. We don't belong to the marine aristocracy. We're just common or garden visitors—(*pointedly*) not good enough for some people.

Bob (*using a shell as a monocle and mimicking a Mayfair accent*) If you don't have a hut at Little-Slippyng-on-Sea you're low common folk, not worth a civil word.

Mom. People who have gone to the expense of renting a beach hut here, expect to be able to sit in front of it in peace and quiet.

Bob. Ladi-bloomin'-da! (*Facing Mom*) What's wrong with people enjoying themselves?

Mom. This has always been a very select place.

Percy (*unhappily; leaning over to Mom*) Look here, Mom, we don't want to say anything we don't mean. (*He smiles at Bob*) I'm sure we all want to just enjoy a nice holiday at the seaside.

(*The* Mother *enters* r *with a piece of seaweed and crosses to* l)

Bob (*sitting round front again; pacified*) Sure, chum. That's all right by me. What I said was just a bit of fun.

(*As* Mother *moves above Noreen to exit* l, *the seaweed touches Noreen's back*)

Mother. As soon as I touched my seaweed, I knew it was gonna be wet.

Foley (*emerging from the hut to between George and Mrs Crum*)

Well, Mrs Crum, you're certainly very fully furnished, as the house agents say.

(PERCY *goes into his hut*)

MRS CRUM. Bide-a-Wee's absolutely our home when we're here. I like nice things.

(GEORGE *does a "winding-up" motion*)

We can have tea here, or lunch. We've got a gramophone— and a portable wireless, and coats and mackintoshes, and sewing things . . . (*She notices George, and stops, glaring*)

(GEORGE *reads his paper*)

FOLEY. Yes, indeed. Hardly got room to get inside your-selves. (*He descends the steps, signs to the Beach Attendant and crosses to below Mom's steps*)

(*The* BEACH ATTENDANT *goes up Beauty's steps to* R *of Mom*)

BEACH ATTENDANT (*reading from a paper*) Ben Nevis—Mrs Gunner—this lady.

(PERCY *comes out of the hut*)

FOLEY. Is this your hut, madam?
MOM. It certainly is.
FOLEY. Mind if I have a look inside?
MOM (*belligerently*) Have you got a search warrant?
BOB. Oi! Oi!
FOLEY (*his eyebrows rising*) No.
MOM. Then you'd better go and get one.
PERCY. I say, Mom . . .
MOM. Be quiet, Percy.
FOLEY. But really, madam, I cannot see why you should object to . . .
MOM. That Lady Beckman! With her mink coats and her Rolls Royce cars! Sending along policemen to poke and pry into people's private huts. It's disgraceful and I won't have it.
PERCY. But look here, Mom . . .
MOM. Will you be quiet, Percy.
BEACH ATTENDANT (*suddenly coming forward to* R *of Mom and speaking persuasively*) Now, madam, be reasonable. It

wouldn't be nice for a lady like you to be seen going to the police station with an officer in order to make a statement, and that's what will happen. Mr Foley here is a very nice gentleman and he just wants to satisfy himself as there's nothing there shouldn't be in your beach hut. Why, you know, mum, it mightn't be an emerald necklace at all. For all you know, it might be a bomb.

(MOM *is slightly shattered by the bomb theory.* GEORGE *lowers his paper.* BOB *laughs*)

MOM. A bomb? But why?

BEACH ATTENDANT. You never know nowadays. (*Looking at Foley*) All this atomic stuff and Communists.

MOM. Very well. (*To Foley; grandly*) You may enter, Inspector.

(*The* BEACH ATTENDANT *straightens up, descends the steps and crosses to below George.* FOLEY *enters Ben Nevis.* PERCY *sits in his chair*)

GEORGE (*to the Beach Attendant*) You're quite a one, aren't you?

BEACH ATTENDANT (*picking up a carton and putting it in the bin down* R) Have to be, in my job. Trouble, trouble, all day long. The ladies are all right if you know how to treat 'em. (*Thoughtfully*) You see a lot of 'uman nature on the beach.

BOB. One thousand pounds reward! Phew! Worth having a shot at it. Good as winning a premium bond or the pools, eh, Artie?

(FOLEY *comes out from the hut and down the steps.*
BEAUTY *comes on down* R *by the telescope and stands watching*)

MR SOMERS. You've got to have brains to do the pools.

(FOLEY *stops above Noreen*)

NOREEN. Coo—if I found an emerald necklace, I'd keep it. (*She sees Foley*) 'Ullo!

FOLEY (*looking at the middle hut*) Mon Desir. (*He crosses to the rostrum*)

BEACH ATTENDANT (*reading from his list*) Ben Nevis, Mrs Gunner. Mong Desser.

(*He mounts the steps of Mon Desir with* FOLEY)

Mrs Murgatroyd, not seen her about lately. Don't suppose anyone's at home. (*He raps on the door*)

(BEAUTY *comes down the steps* R *by the telescope*)

BEAUTY. Ye-es? You want something please?

(GEORGE *looks at her*)

I can do something?
    MRS CRUM. George!
    BEACH ATTENDANT. This is Mrs Murgatroyd's hut?
    BEAUTY (*nodding vigorously, and coming below* R *of the steps of Mon Desir*) Oh, yes. She is friend of my aunt's. She say to me, I can use her hut. She give me ze key. (*She holds out the key, taking it from her bra*)
    FOLEY (*taking it*) Oh! I am Inspector Foley. Will you allow me to inspect . . .
    BEAUTY. You are inspector? Yes? You do not like my costume? (*Looking down at herself*) Is not enough? No?
    GEORGE. Yes.
    BOB. Mamselle, it's perfect.
    BEACH ATTENDANT. It's not your costume, miss. We're broad-minded here, not like some beaches. You see, there has been a robbery, and the Inspector here thinks—er—something may have been put in your hut.
    BEAUTY. I do not understand. Who put in my hut? What?
    GEORGE. An emerald necklace.
    BEAUTY. An emerald necklace! In my hut? Why? C'n'est pas possible. Je ne pense pas comprendre. Qui l'aurait faite, une belle chose. Mais c'est complètement fou.
    GEORGE. Yes—well—er—yes.
    FOLEY. Mademoiselle—vous—you permit me to enter?
    BEAUTY. Oh, yes, I permit. (*She sits* R *of the steps of Mon Desir*)

(FOLEY *enters Mon Desir.* BEAUTY *drops her sun-glasses.* PERCY *retrieves them for her*)

(*Giving him a warm smile*) Oh, thank you. You are very kind.
    PERCY (*embarrassed and pleased*) Don't mention it. (*He sits* L *of the steps of Mon Desir*)

BEAUTY (*to Percy*) You have been in the sea? It is very cold.

PERCY. No, not at all. I mean, yes, it is.

BEAUTY. But you are braver, perhaps, than I am. If the water is cold I am not brave.

(FOLEY *comes out to* L *of the hut. The* BEACH ATTENDANT *stands at* R *of him*)

FOLEY. Not much in there.

BEAUTY. No, there is very little. Some very ugly cups and saucers and a tin of tea, and plain, plain English biscuits. I do not like your English biscuits.

MOM (*to Percy; sharply*) Percy, get your clothes on. You'll die of cold.

PERCY (*fascinated by Beauty, who is smiling at him*) What? Oh, yes!

MR SOMERS. Yes, it is getting chilly.

NOREEN (*rising; sharply*) Well, if the excitement's over, what about a run along the beach? Coming, Bob? 'Bye, Arthur.

(NOREEN *exits* L)

BOB (*rising and turning to Beauty*) Well, au revoy, eh? (*Still watching Beauty, he starts crossing* L)

(NOREEN *returns down* L. BOB *bumps into her*)

NOREEN. Come on then, Bob!

BOB (*reluctantly*) Coming. Just having a parlez-vous with this bird here . . .

NOREEN. Just 'cos she's French . . . !

(NOREEN *pushes* BOB, *and they exit down* L)

FOLEY. Sorry you've been troubled.

(FOLEY *exits up the ramp and to up* L.
MR SOMERS *rises with difficulty, using his sticks. The* BEACH ATTENDANT *crosses* L *to him*)

BEACH ATTENDANT. Give you a hand, sir?

MR SOMERS (*crossing* R) I can manage. (*He raises his hat when* L *of Beauty*) Bon jour!

(MR SOMERS *exits down* R. *The* BEACH ATTENDANT *exits down* L)

BEAUTY. Poor man. (*She opens her cigarette-case and takes
a cigarette out*) Oh—please—will you be very kind?
PERCY (*rising to L of Beauty*) Of course, yes, anything.
BEAUTY. My lighter, she has packed up.

(GEORGE *rises, taking his lighter out.* PERCY *crosses to R
of Beauty, takes George's lighter, and lights her cigarette*)

Thank you.
MOM. Get your clothes on, Percy. It's cold!
PERCY. My clothes? Oh—yes . . . (*He moves on to the
rostrum to enter Ben Nevis*)
GEORGE. Oi, Romeo! (*He holds out his hand*)

(PERCY *dashes back, returns George's lighter, crosses to the
deck-chair, picks up Bob's trousers and his own shirt, and goes
into the hut, closing the door behind him.*

GEORGE *sits again.* BEAUTY *hums a little tune.* GEORGE
watches her avidly. MRS CRUM *and* MOM *look at each other.*
BEAUTY *looks at George and smiles*)

MRS CRUM (*packing away her knitting and rising with deter-
mination*) Come on, George, we'll go along to the kiosk
and have a cup of tea.
GEORGE. Don't think I want any tea.
MRS CRUM. We'll go along to the kiosk and have a cup of
tea, George.
GEORGE. Will we? All right, then.

(MRS CRUM *leans on George's knee to descend the steps*)

Oh! Blimey!
MRS CRUM. Give us a hand down, can't you?

(GEORGE *helps her down the steps. When she has passed
Beauty,* MRS CRUM *adjusts her girdle, and crosses on to the
ramp*)

(*From the ramp*) Are you coming, Mrs Gunner?
MOM (*obviously longing for tea, but not wanting to leave Percy
and Beauty together*) Well, in a minute perhaps.
MRS CRUM. The kiosk shuts at five.
BEAUTY (*rising*) I think I shall go now and take a bath.

(BEAUTY *takes her bathing-cap and crosses to exit down L.*

PERCY *comes out of the hut, wearing shirt and trousers, and stares after Beauty)*

MOM (*rising; sharply*) Mrs Crum and I are going to have a cup of tea.

PERCY. Right you are. (*He moves down to the bottom of the ramp*) I don't want any. I'll go for a stroll. (*He prepares to start after Beauty)*

MOM. No, Percy, you'll stay here until we come back. Do you understand? Don't move from here. Anything might be taken.

(PERCY *moves* C, *to* R *of the sand castle)*

It's bad enough ordinary days, and with all these cat burglars and dangerous characters about, you can't be too careful. Look after Mr and Mrs Crum's things too.

PERCY. Oh, all right.

(GEORGE *comes to behind Percy, both looking after Beauty)*

MOM (*as she and Mrs Crum move up the ramp*) I'm not going to that place we went to yesterday. My cup was covered in lipstick. I didn't like the girl, either.

(MOM *and* MRS CRUM *go off up* L. GEORGE *moves after them, but turns first and winks at Percy)*

GEORGE. Good luck, my boy.

(PERCY *looks at him miserably.* GEORGE *moves to the ramp, looks off up* L, *then returns to* L *of Percy.*
The light starts to fade a little)

Look here, Percy, my boy, you stand up for yourself before it's too late.

PERCY. What do you mean?

GEORGE. There's such a thing as being *too* nice to your mother. All very well in its way, but you can go too far. Assert yourself. Be a man.

MRS CRUM (*off*) George!

GEORGE. Coming!

(GEORGE *exits up* L. PERCY *sits by himself on the beach, staring miserably in front of him. He feels in his right-hand trouser pocket for a cigarette, then, still abstractedly, in his left-hand pocket. He frowns, feeling with his fingers, and slowly draws out a gleaming emerald necklace. He stares at it for a moment uncomprehendingly, then a look of horror passes over his face. He looks sharply up and down the beach, shoves the necklace back in his pocket, takes it out again, and stares at it. Then he rises, goes up the ramp* L, *returns to the beach, looks off* L, *and looks at Mon Desir)*

NOREEN (*off* L) Come on, Bob, don't take all day.

BOB (*off* L) I've dropped me towel.

(PERCY *shoves the necklace back in his pocket and sits* C *abruptly.*

NOREEN *enters down* L)

NOREEN. C'mon, I'll beat you, Bob. You're out of condition. Too many cigarettes.

BOB (*off* L) Only forty a day.

(PERCY *kneels on the sand*)

NOREEN. Blimey, I'm out of breath!

(PERCY *does not answer. She looks at him*)

Hullo—anything the matter?

PERCY. No—yes.

NOREEN (L *of Percy*) Well, make up your mind. I'd better get dressed, I suppose. (*She goes to the sand castle for her towel, then faces the rostrum* C) Dressing and undressing on a beach is a regular art, I must say. At the critical moment the towel always slips. (*She slips her shoulder-straps off and tucks the towel under her arms*)

(BOB *enters* L, *panting*)

BOB. Oh!

NOREEN. Go away, Bob. You'll have to wait until I'm Mrs Respectable. At the moment I'm liable to be Mrs Rude any minute.

BOB. Pardon me, I'm sure. Sing out when you're decent. Where's old Arthur? Oh, I see him, doing his constitutional over there.

(BOB *crosses and exits down* R)

PERCY (*to himself*) Wish I knew what to do.

NOREEN. Pardon? (*Letting the towel slip off her left shoulder*) Oh, drat this towel. You—Mister . . .

PERCY. Percy Gunner.

NOREEN. Yes, hang on! (*She holds out the end of the towel*)

(PERCY *takes it,* R *of her*)

That's it, just keep it from slipping. (*She wriggles a good deal. The towel slips*) Where's me clothes? (*She moves above the deck-chair, picks up her dress and places it on the rostrum*) Where's me . . . (*She goes to her beach bag above the deck-chair*) Bra! Bra! Bra! (*She takes out her bra, crosses and puts it on top of her dress*) Oh, here, give it to me. (*She takes the towel from Percy*) You must keep watch. (*She starts to dry herself, then notices Percy watching her*) Well, don't watch *me!* Watch out for men.

(PERCY *moves* RC, *looking off* R)

(*She dries herself, then takes her bra and shakes it*) Blimey, it's full of sand! (*She puts on her bra*) Can't find the bloomin' hook. Here, Percy, hang on. Both ends. (*Giving him the towel*)

(PERCY *holds the towel, facing front*)

(*She fastens the hook, and slips into her dress. Then she steps out from behind the towel*) Olé!

(PERCY *drops the towel*)

(*Turning to face* L) Zip me up, ducks, will you?

(PERCY *goes to her and tries to zip the dress*)

Wicked things, zips. Here, take it by surprise.

(PERCY *zips the dress*)

Don't forget the hook at the top.

(PERCY *fastens the hook at the top of the dress*)

Not very used to this sort of thing, are you? You're looking very serious! Anything the matter? (*She struggles out of her costume*)

PERCY. Wish I knew what to do.

NOREEN. Where's me Kleenex? (*She drops the costume on the sand, goes to her handbag, kneels, takes out a Kleenex, and blows her nose*) Now, what's the matter with you, ducks? (*She takes a mirror and comb from her bag and combs her hair*)

PERCY (*moving to* R *of Noreen and showing her the necklace*) Look! I've just found this in my trouser pocket.

NOREEN (*stopping combing and staring at it*) What on earth —you mean—is this the necklace that all the fuss is about?

PERCY. I should think it must be. Don't you?

NOREEN. And you found it in your—what do you mean, *found* it? Didn't you know it was there?

PERCY. I hadn't the least idea.

NOREEN. You mean, you didn't put it there yourself?

PERCY. Of course I didn't! It wasn't there just now— before I went to bathe.

NOREEN. You mean—someone put it there.

PERCY. They must have.

NOREEN. But who? But who? (*She gives a sharp glance round at the huts and the beach*) Oh, I see . . .

PERCY. What d'you mean?

NOREEN (*going to her beach bag and taking out her drawers*) Where's me drawers? (*Shaking them*) Sand everywhere! (*She puts them on*)

(*The* YOUNG MAN *enters down* L *with the ball as Noreen has her drawers round her ankles. He whistles and exits* L.

NOREEN *turns* R *as Percy is watching.* PERCY *turns* R, *while* NOREEN *faces up stage and pulls up her drawers*)

PERCY. You said "you see". What do you see?

NOREEN (*slowly, as though trying to puzzle something out, as she kneels by the sand castle and combs her hair*) Of course. *She* must have put it there.

PERCY. She? You mean . . .

NOREEN. The Pin-up Girl from Mon Desir.

PERCY. No! I don't believe it.

NOREEN. Only way it could have happened. Your clothes were on the beach, weren't they? The police came along. I suppose she had it with her in that bathing bag. When they started to search your hut, she shoved it in your trouser pocket.

PERCY. Yes—yes—I suppose that's how it must have happened.

NOREEN. Well, cheer up. (*She drops the comb and rises to* L *of Percy*) 'Ere, you take it along to the inspector chap and you'll get the reward—a thousand pounds, just think of that.

PERCY. And she'll go to prison.

NOREEN. Oh, I see. (*She thumps him on the chest*) Don't you be a sucker, Percy. That girl must be in with the gang. The cat burglar steals the things and shoves it in the hut, and she comes along and picks it up next day.

PERCY (*unwillingly*) Yes, I suppose it must have been like that. (*Looking off down* L) But she's so young. *breather*

NOREEN. Probably been at it ever since she was a kiddy. Their mums teach 'em to shoplift when they're children.

(BOB *enters down* L *and goes to above the deck-chair for his sweater*)

BOB (*crossly*) Don't care if I die of cold, do you? Why didn't you shout when you were ready?

NOREEN. Bob, you'll never guess! What d'you think Mister—Percy . . . ?

PERCY. Percy Gunner.

NOREEN. What d'you think he's got? (*She takes the necklace from Percy and crosses to* R *of Bob*) Hold your breath, count three, and don't say anything you'd be sorry for afterwards. (*She holds up the necklace*)

(As BOB's *head comes through his sweater he sees the necklace*)

BOB (*bereft of speech for a moment*) Well—blimey! Cor stone the crows! Where did that come from?

NOREEN. Found it in his trouser pocket, see? I tell him someone must have put it there.

BOB (*a little dazed*) Someone must have put it there—who?

NOREEN. The girl, of course. The foreign girl. It couldn't have been anyone else. You agree, don't you? It must have been that girl.

BOB (*sitting in the deck-chair and combing his hair*) Oh, yes, undoubtedly—the girl.

PERCY (*explosively*) No!

BOB (*looking at Percy as he parts his hair*) But it stands to reason, old man.

PERCY. No—I don't believe it. I won't believe it!

NOREEN (*moving to* L *of Percy*) You men—you're all the same. Here she is—coming now. (*She moves above the deck-chair*)

(BEAUTY *enters* L. *She is not wet. She crosses to Percy.*
PERCY *puts her cape on*)

BEAUTY (*smiling*) Oh, thank you. It is cold, the water. I
put one toe in, so—(*she demonstrates*) and I say *no!* I . . .
(*She stops as she sees the necklace. There is a pause, then she goes
on with a slight change of voice*) Ah, you have my necklace
there.

BOB. Are you telling us that's your's?

BEAUTY. But yes—of course!

PERCY. But—it was stolen.

BEAUTY (*laughing*) Ah—I see. You think it is *that* necklace. No, it is mine. It is—how do you say—costume
jewellery. (*She crosses to Noreen and takes the necklace from her
quickly. She clasps it round her neck, and turns to Percy*) It looks
nice, yes? (*She turns to Noreen*) Where did you find it?

PERCY. It was in my pocket.

BEAUTY (*surprised*) In *your* pocket? You took it? But why?

PERCY. I didn't take it.

BEAUTY (*gently*) I see. You did not know you took it.
Yes, I have heard of that—klop—m—kleptomania. You
cannot help it. See, I have my necklace back and nothing
more shall be said about it. (*She goes up the* C *steps on to the
rostrum*)

BOB (*sharply and with an ugly manner*) No!

(BEAUTY *stops and turns enquiringly*)

No, you don't. (*He rises and goes on to the rostrum,* L *of Beauty*)

BEAUTY. What do you want?

BOB. You're not going to get away with that necklace.

PERCY (*suddenly looking down at his legs*) Wait a minute!
These aren't my trousers. (*He crosses to the deck-chair*) I
had cigarettes in my trousers. (*To Bob*) *Those* are my
trousers. These are your's. It was in your pocket.

BOB (*menacingly; to Beauty*) Hand that over—quick.

BEAUTY. No, I will not.

(PERCY *advances on him.* BOB *snatches the necklace from
Beauty and runs down on to the beach.* BEAUTY *trips him up
and he falls on the sand down* R, *dropping the necklace.*
FOLEY *enters down* R *to above* R *of Bob.* MR SOMERS
enters down R *to* R *of Bob.* NOREEN *crosses to* L *of Foley, who*

picks up the necklace. PERCY *crosses to below* L *of Noreen.* BEAUTY *comes down the centre steps)*

FOLEY. Keep him there!

BOB		Oh, my knee! I've broken something!
BEAUTY		*(speaking now without a foreign accent)* It was in his trouser pocket. The other gentleman put the wrong trousers on.
	(together)	
PERCY		I picked up the wrong trousers.
MR SOMERS		What's going on here?
NOREEN		I don't understand—what's happening?

NOREEN. Arthur, it's the necklace. Lady Beckman's, the stolen one. It seems to have been in Bob's pocket.

BOB. It's a frame-up, I tell you.

NOREEN. I can't believe it. I just can't believe it.

MR SOMERS. Bob?

FOLEY *(to Noreen)* How well do you know this man?

MR SOMERS. Only met him since we came down here—a week ago.

NOREEN. Staying at the same guest-house.

MR SOMERS. Seemed a very pleasant, agreeable chap. We've got in the habit of going about together.

FOLEY. Just so.

NOREEN. I can't believe it. Bob—a cat burglar.

BOB *(rising)* It's all a mistake, I tell you! Someone put that necklace in my pocket. It's a frame-up.

FOLEY. You can explain all that at the station. Get your clothes!

(BOB *rises and crosses to above the deck-chair.* FOLEY *moves to above the sand castle, patting Percy on the back in passing)*

Good piece of work, my boy. Looks as though you may be the richer by a thousand pounds.

BOB. These aren't my trousers.

PERCY. Wait a minute. *(He takes off the trousers he is wearing)*

FOLEY *(handing Bob's shoes to him, and taking the trousers from him)* Are these your shoes?

PERCY (*holding up the trousers in front of him*) You do understand, don't you, that this young lady had nothing whatever to do with it? Excuse me!

FOLEY (*grinning*) I'd better introduce you.

(GEORGE *and* MRS CRUM *enter up* L *and move to the foot of the ramp*)

This is Policewoman Alice Jones.

(PERCY *drops the trousers.* FOLEY *and* PERCY *exchange the trouser pairs via* BEAUTY)

Good work, Jones. You tripped him very neatly.

BEAUTY. Thank you, sir.

FOLEY. On your way!

BOB. French policewoman on an English beach. I'll see my shop steward about this!

(FOLEY *and* BOB *exit by the ramp up* L)

PERCY. Policewoman Alice Jones!

BEAUTY. Yes.

MR SOMERS (*crossing below Percy and Beauty to sit in the deck-chair*) You could have fooled me.

PERCY. You were on duty?

BEAUTY. Yes.

PERCY. You—you don't look like a policewoman.

(NOREEN *crosses between Percy and Beauty to* L *of the sand castle, kneels, and collects her things*)

BEAUTY. I'm not supposed to.

PERCY. And what do you do next?

BEAUTY. Well—I've got the rest of the day off.

PERCY. Look here—would—could you—come and have something to eat at the Pavilion and then go to a show afterwards?

BEAUTY. I'd love to.

(MOM *enters, to the up* L *edge of the rostrum*)

I'll just get some clothes on. (*She enters her hut to dress and closes the door*)

PERCY. Oh, yes! (*He puts on his trousers*)

MRS CRUM (*crossing to* R *of Mom's chair*) That girl—she's a policewoman!

Mom (*going to her chair*) Percy, what is all this? What has been going on?

PERCY. I've recovered Lady Beckman's emerald necklace.

MRS CRUM. Well, would you believe it?

GEORGE (*crossing below the rostrum to his steps*) So you recovered it, did you? That's a thousand pounds in your pocket, me boy. Hope you're allowed to spend it.

Mom. A thousand pounds.

GEORGE (*sitting in Mrs Crum's chair*) Nothing like a bit of money to give you independence.

PERCY. It's not the money I'm thinking about. It's Miss . . .

Mom. Percy, what did you say to that girl?

PERCY. I asked her to go to the Pavilion with me.

Mom. Nonsense. You can't do that. You don't know her.

PERCY. I'll know her better soon.

GEORGE. I bet you will.

MRS CRUM. George!

(PERCY *moves up the ramp* L)

Mom. Oh, dear! This has all been too much for me. I think I've got one of my headaches coming on. (*She sinks on to her chair*)

(MRS CRUM *snatches Mom's knitting from her chair just before she sits on it*)

MRS CRUM. Whoops!

NOREEN. We'd better go home. (*She moves below Mr Somers on to the ramp*) Bob a cat burglar! I can't believe it. Coming, Arthur?

MR SOMERS. In a minute, dear. You go on.

NOREEN (*nudging Percy*) Here, Percy, you know what you've got to do. Stick to your guns, Gunner!

(NOREEN *exits up the ramp to up* L)

MRS CRUM. Come and see to your mother, Percy. She looks real bad to me.

PERCY (*moving to* L *of Mom*) Are you all right, Mom?

Mom. It's my heart.

GEORGE. Here we go again.

PERCY. Where are your smelling salts? (*He takes the salts from her bag and thrusts them under her nose*)

(MOM *waves the salts away*)

GEORGE. Here, fan her with this.

(PERCY *crosses to take George's paper and fans Mom's right ear, which she covers. Then he crosses to* L *of her.*
The MOTHER *enters* R, *crossing to* L)

MOTHER. Ernie! Bert! Come along the two of you, we've got to catch our bus.
MOM. Oh, that woman!
MOTHER. Ernie!
MOM. That voice!
MOTHER. I won't 'alf give it to you when I get hold of you. Ernie! ! !

(*The* MOTHER *exits* L.
BEAUTY *comes out of the hut*)

BEAUTY. All ready now.
PERCY. I'm sorry—it's . . .

(BEAUTY *closes the door of the hut*)

I mean—my mother isn't feeling very well.
MOM. I'm sorry to be such a drag on you, my dear boy, but I really feel *quite* queer.
PERCY (*stopping fanning*) Perhaps—(*looking appealingly at Mrs Crum*) you'd be kind enough to . . . (*He stops*)
MOM (*to Beauty*) You'll understand I'm sure, Miss— er . . .
BEAUTY. Jones. Alice Jones.
MOM. Miss Jones. I'm so sorry—but I really have a very bad headache and I feel rather faint.

(PERCY *fans again*)

BEAUTY (*briskly*) That's too bad, isn't it. I know just what you need—rest. Men are useless when you're feeling ill, aren't they? (*She crosses down the steps to the ramp*) Come on, Percy, we'll leave your mother to be peaceful.
PERCY. Mom . . .
MOM. Oh, dear. (*She closes her eyes*)
BEAUTY (*to Percy*) Well? (*She waits*)

PERCY. I . . .

BEAUTY. Well, good-bye, all. (*She goes up the ramp*)

(BEAUTY *exits up* L)

PERCY. Wait! Miss Jones . . . (*He gives the paper to Mrs Crum*)

(PERCY *exits up the ramp up* L)

GEORGE. Good boy! Oh, good boy!

(MRS CRUM *sits in Percy's chair and fans Mom*)

MOM. That I should ever live to see this day. My own boy going off and leaving me in that callous way. That horrid girl. Policewoman indeed.

MRS CRUM (*fanning herself*) Poor dear, I feel for you. I really do.

MOM (*rising*) Well, I'm not going to sit around. I shall go home—if I can make it on my own.

MRS CRUM (*rising to* L *of her chair*) I'll come with you.

MOM. Leaving me to close up Ben Nevis on my own, too. I'm not used to it.

MRS CRUM. George!

(GEORGE *puts down his paper and crosses to stow away the chairs into Ben Nevis*)

MOM. It's not a bit like my Percy. I don't know what's come over him.

GEORGE (*folding the chairs*) I do.

MOM. See that everything's in.

(GEORGE *puts away the second chair, crosses to his own chair, and picks up his paper*)

If you'd be so kind, Mr Crum.

(GEORGE *crosses back, takes the key from Mom and locks the hut*)

Have you locked up properly?

GEORGE. Here's your key. (*He gives her the key*) I suppose we'd better take you home.

MOM. Oh, yes, take me home. (*She goes up the ramp*)

(MRS CRUM *follows*)

Everybody knows I might die any minute. Nobody cares whether I live or die.

MRS CRUM. No, George, we don't need you.

(MRS CRUM *and* MOM *exit up* L)

GEORGE (*crossing along the rostrum to his hut*) Women!

MR SOMERS. As you say—women.

(GEORGE *packs up his chairs and places them in the hut. The* BEACH ATTENDANT *enters down* L, *crosses to down* R, *picks up a carton and puts it in the basket, discovers a bra, picks it up, notices George has put his chairs in the hut and is about to descend his steps*)

BEACH ATTENDANT. Wireless says it's gonna rain to-morrow. They'll be wrong. Never known them right yet. Be another blasted fine day.

GEORGE (*looking at the bra*) Not mine.

(*The* BEACH ATTENDANT *exits down* L. GEORGE *crosses to* R *of the sand castle*)

MR SOMERS. Ah, well! (*He rises, stretches his legs, goes to the sand castle, extracts the necklace from it and hands it to George*) Here you are, old man.

GEORGE. So you had it all the time! But what was the other one?

MR SOMERS. Oh, that was the replica. No time to leave it last night. Blasted chambermaid came along two hours after she was supposed to go off duty. Putting it in Bob's pocket was Noreen's little bit of fun.

GEORGE. Noreen's sense of fun will go too far one day. Poor old Bob.

MR SOMERS. Well, somebody's got to be the fall guy. A good deal too fresh for my liking. Needs to be taught a lesson. He's cut out for the part. (*He moves to above the deck-chair*) He's got a record, you know.

GEORGE. Whereas we—I'm a respectable working jeweller. Don't look like a fence, do I?

MR SOMERS. And I don't look like a cat burglar, do I? (*He sits in the deck-chair*)

(GEORGE *goes to his hut to close the doors and lock up*)

MRS CRUM (*off*) George!

(MRS CRUM *enters up* L)

Come on, George. Are you going to stay on the beach all night? That Mrs Gunner's in a terrible state.

MRS GEORGE (*locking the hut*) Serve the old trout right.

MRS CRUM. Eh? I tell you one thing. (*She moves to* L *of the rostrum*) I'm not coming back to this place next year.

GEORGE (*ambling after her*) Perhaps you're right, dear. Mustn't go to the same place too often.

MR SOMERS. Excuse me, have you got a light?

(GEORGE *comes down to the beach and lights a cigarette for Mr Somers*)

MRS CRUM. Next year I shall go to Clacton-on-Sea.

(MRS CRUM *exits up* L)

GEORGE. Clacton-on-Sea. Yes, I think you've got something there. Clacton. Yes, that will do very nicely.

GEORGE *exits up* L.

MR SOMERS *crosses his game leg, and tilts his hat. The lights dim to a* BLACK-OUT.

CURTAIN

Lights out + on

FURNITURE AND PROPERTY PLOT

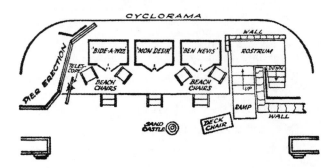

On stage: BIDE-A-WEE:

    Top shelf: 3 boxes, flask, Frugrains, Ovaltine, blue tin, paintbrush, saucers, box

    Lower shelf: jug, plates, cups, bowl, saucers, jam, coffee, tins, cigarette packet, glass, jug, mayonnaise, cutlery, roses, paper bag, teapot, Silvikrin, glass, boxes, rusks, battery and flex

    Line R: tablecloth. L: bra, 2 scarves

    On hooks: tea-towel, carrier bag, mackintosh

    On floor: washing-bowl, box, towel-rail, hat, 2 tins of paint, 2 pairs of shoes, paper bags

    In front: 2 camp-chairs, knitting bag L, newspaper R

    Doors, open

    Padlock on R door

MON DESIR

    L *side:* hooks, mirror (for quick change)

    Top shelf: magazine, tin, 5 books

    Lower shelf: pad, 3 saucers, teapot, 3 cups (hanging)

    On floor: broken camp-chair

    Doors, closed

    Padlock, open

BEN NEVIS:

    L *side:* 2 camp-chairs, necklace on hook downstage corner

Top shelf: jug, ball, saucepan, bowl, 2 saucers, 2 sweet boxes
On wall: postcard
On hooks: tea-towel, 2 cups
On floor: 2 boxes, magazine, red socks
Doors, closed with padlock, but not snapped shut
Deck-chair down L. *On it:* newspaper, stick
Behind it: Noreen's dress, Bob's trousers, sweater and comb
Sand castle down C
  In it: necklace
  On it: rubber bucket, box with one chocolate
  L *of it:* red towel, Noreen's shoes, pink bag with pants and bra, bathing cap, handbag with Kleenex, mirror, comb
  R *of it:* Bob's towel, shoes, rubber shell, 2 shells
Telescope R. *On it:* litter basket ($\frac{1}{4}$ full)

In R *wing*: Bra, two pieces of rubbish

Off stage L: Beach ball, Percy's towel

Off stage R: Seaweed

On kiosk L: *Upstage flap:* postcards
    Downstage flap: 2 balls, 4 buckets; 5 spades

Personal: Lighter (GEORGE)
Beach bag with sun-glasses, packet with 2 cigarettes (plain), lighter (no flint), bathing cap, key to Mon Desir (BEAUTY)
Bag with knitting, handbag with smelling-salts, key to Ben Nevis (MOM)
Packet with 3 cigarettes, matches, florin (MR SOMERS)
Handbag (MRS CRUM)
Tickets, ticket-clipper, money bag with 2 pennies, sixpence, shilling, hut list, whistle, watch and chain (BEACH ATTENDANT)

LIGHTING PLOT

Property fittings required: none

Exterior. A beach

THE APPARENT SOURCE OF LIGHT is the sun

THE MAIN ACTING AREAS are up RC, up C, up LC, RC, C
and LC

A summer afternoon

To open: BLACK-OUT

Cue 1	At rise of CURTAIN *Fade up daylight*	(Page 1)
Cue 2	GEORGE: "Good luck, my boy." *Daylight fades a little*	(Page 21)
Cue 3	At end of Play *Dim to* BLACK-OUT	(Page 33)

EFFECTS PLOT

Cue 1	BOB: "Keep Britain tidy." *Jet plane flying overhead running into: Barking dog*	(Page 2)
Cue 2	YOUNG MAN: "Sorry, sorry." *Fade barking dog*	(Page 2)
Cue 3	NOREEN: "Here, Bob, sit down." *Dog fight*	(Page 12)
Cue 4	MOTHER: ". . . a naughty boy. Ernie!" *Dog fight stops*	(Page 12)
Cue 5	GEORGE: ". . . beside the seaside." *Jet plane flying overhead, roars twice then fast fade to out*	(Page 13)

MADE AND PRINTED IN GREAT BRITAIN BY
LATIMER TREND & COMPANY LTD PLYMOUTH

MADE IN ENGLAND